A GARDENER'S JOURNAL

A GARDENER'S JOURNAL

Penelope Hobhouse

THE ART & PRACTICE OF GARDENING

Principal photography by Ted Betz

WILLOW CREEK PRESS

MINOCQUA, WISCONSIN

Penelope Hobhouse: The Art & Practice of Gardening was produced by
Perennial Productions for Home & Garden Television

A Gardener's Journal
© Frances Lincoln Limited 1997
Text © Penelope Hobhouse 1997
The copyright in the photographs is the property of the
photographers as listed on the last page of this journal.

A Gardener's Journal was conceived, edited and designed by
Frances Lincoln Limited, 4 Torriano Mews, Torriano Avenue,
London NW5 2RZ

Published in the U.S.A. by WILLOW CREEK PRESS
P.O. Box 147, Minocqua, Wisconsin 54548. 1-800-850-9453

ISBN 1 57223 108 4

Set in Bell Mt
Printed and bound in Hong Kong by Paramount Printing Co. Ltd

9 8 7 6 5 4 3 2 1

Frontispiece *The inner walled garden at Bettiscombe is laid out very simply on two levels connected by three sets of steps. In the upper area, formal trees, rose arches, and evergreen phillyreas frame pathways laid out on a grid system, with climbers curtaining all the walls. On the lower level, a gravel garden and pots are filled with Mediterranean-type plants, many of which are luxuriant self-seeders.*

Right *Purple alliums,* Erysimum *'Bowles' Mauve' and drifts of allium-related creamy nectaroscordums are planted in the Walled Garden at Hadspen. The wide borders around the edge of the garden are filled with different color schemes and combinations, usually planted in quite broad sweeps, which provide interest from spring to late autumn.*

INTRODUCTION

Gardening is a fine art – you need a painter's eye for color and composition, an architect's sense of proportion and symmetry, and a sculptor's feel for manipulating form and texture in three dimensions. Gardening is also a continuous learning process and the principles with which I introduce each month of this journal are similar to the guidelines artists are given, so as to develop their own style and technique. Making quite detailed notes of what does and doesn't work in the garden is vital to personal development. Writing things down always concentrates the mind and is the first step towards remembering, even if you never look at your notes again. The notes remain available as a quick aide memoire to the way you garden as well as a record of the progressions of the seasons.

In my own garden, where the outline planning is almost complete, my notes cover planting associations and horticultural matters such as ordering bulbs or sowing annuals and reminders to prune or mulch. In other people's gardens, style, features, architecture and planting schemes are all worth looking at and recording. I like to measure steps, pace out distances, look at the skyline, note color associations.

I make a record of good things and bad, of brilliant innovative ideas and those which haven't come off because the style, scale or use of plants is wrong. Of course gardening is a very positive occupation and there should not be too many rules of "do" or "do not" but the best ideas as well as the glaring mistakes can be recognized and then copied or avoided.

As well as writing down garden matters and notes on good plants I see at horticultural shows, I use a journal to record important statements I come across in gardening books and magazines. Sometimes I find that a sentence or phrase just hits the spot, sorting out a puzzle or sending my mind off on new tracks.

Your own notes will reveal your personal learning process and transform this journal into an essential gardening tool.

Penelope Hobhouse

JANUARY

Training your eye I believe that visiting historic gardens and looking at the old formal ways of gardening is an essential prelude to making your own garden or designing for other people. There does exist a "grammar" of design and if you learn this first, from looking and reading, you can adapt the principles to a geometric layout or to freer more naturalistic concepts. Train your eye to notice how space is transformed with associated buildings and plants. In spring at Barnsley House, the classical eighteenth-century temple is framed by yellow ribbons of marsh marigolds, *Caltha palustris*, introducing a quite formal note to the waterside planting.

In the new gravel area in my own walled garden at Bettiscombe, blowsy peony-flowered opium poppies bloom from seed scattered during the winter to complement a more permanent planting of silver-leaved Stachys byzantina, *its violet flower spikes produced in the same season. The shapes, forms, colors, and textures of different plant associations fill in the detail of any overall scheme and every gardener needs to develop the ability to envision these effects from the beginning.*

Train your eye to appreciate the value of framed axial views, which hold a design together. At West Dean, the giant pergola, designed by Harold Peto, has been restored recently and now roses and clematis clamber luxuriantly around the pillars and over the wooden cross bars to highlight the pavilion at the end of the vista.

In any planting scheme the eye seeks for definition and repetition. Most designs, however natural the planting, benefit from strong outlines and solid blocks of color which hold the overall concept together. At Forde Abbey, Irish yews, trimmed as pillars, complement the seventeenth-century canal and link house and garden.

Some plants have architectural qualities of flower or leaf which can be as important as any landscape features. In the cool border at Hadspen, white-flowered tobacco, Nicotiana sylvestris, *although only an annual, soars to six feet or two metres in a few months. With wide green leaves and evening-scented flowers, it plays an important design role in the late summer garden.*

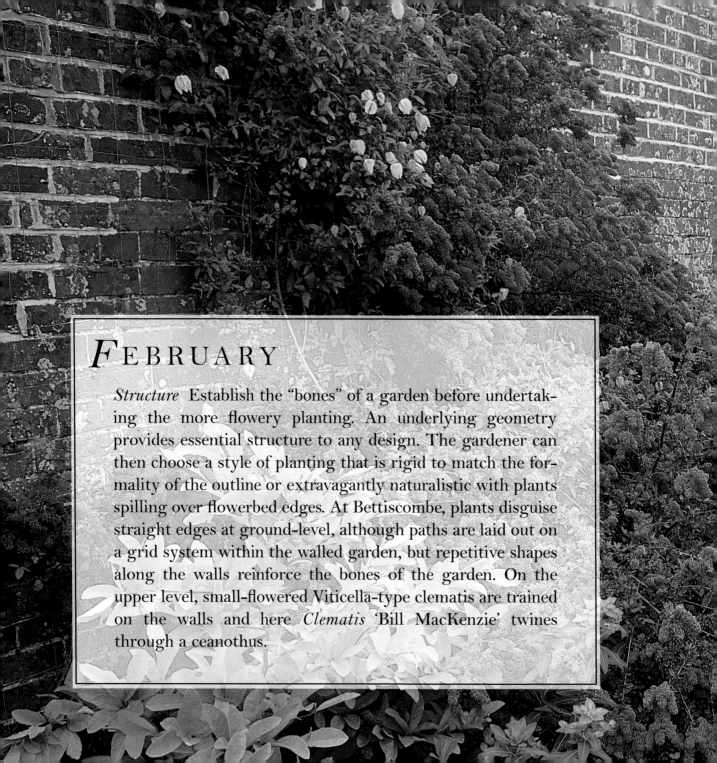

FEBRUARY

Structure Establish the "bones" of a garden before undertaking the more flowery planting. An underlying geometry provides essential structure to any design. The gardener can then choose a style of planting that is rigid to match the formality of the outline or extravagantly naturalistic with plants spilling over flowerbed edges. At Bettiscombe, plants disguise straight edges at ground-level, although paths are laid out on a grid system within the walled garden, but repetitive shapes along the walls reinforce the bones of the garden. On the upper level, small-flowered Viticella-type clematis are trained on the walls and here *Clematis* 'Bill MacKenzie' twines through a ceanothus.

Swaying grasses line a sensuous curving path, crisply mown on one side to provide contrast with the naturalistic flowerbed planting, in this Oehme and van Sweden garden on Chesapeake Bay. This sort of simple yet structured design provides new horizons in American garden styles, reflecting natural rather than man-made structures.

On a frosty morning at Barnsley House, strong structural lines made by dark cylindrically shaped yews (part of the Yew Walk) contrast with the horizontal lawn and the spreading juniper. In winter the bare bones of a garden show through clearly and the underlying design is revealed.

In the manicured gardens at Longwood, structure is given by patterned beds of different colored tulips in spring. Curving spaces, backed by plantings of hardy perennials for later summer performance, are formalized with pyramids of clipped yew that emphasize the outline of the design.

Helen Dillon's garden in Dublin is divided up into a series of structured rooms, each area featuring a different design or planting scheme. A pattern of clipped boxwood surrounds gravel and the central statue but side beds overflowing with lady's mantle (Alchemilla mollis) *soften the formal effects.*

MARCH

Foliage Significance Leaves, with their subtlety of shape, color and texture, play as important a role as flowers in the garden. Flowers have a brief few weeks of bloom while foliage effects last for at least six months and sometimes throughout the gardening year, giving the garden a matrix of muted shades and tints, cool and restful on their own or, by contrast, accentuating glowing flower colors. Choose plants with interesting leaf shapes to provide architectural effects, to soften hard stone edging, and to frame naturalistic water features. At Hadspen, a collection of rodgersias demonstrates variability in shape and texture.

At Winterthur, native ferns and other woodland plants grow beneath the spreading branches of a Japanese maple. Here the usual gardening emphasis on flowers is subordinate to the graphic outline made by the tree, its elegant leaves, and the quiet planting at the base of its trunk.

Ferns, lady's mantle, and topiary box frame the approach to a doorway and a view of glaucous-leaved hostas at Wollerton Old Hall. Flowers become welcome incidents in their season but the success of the whole scheme depends on the different leaf colors and textures.

A mound of golden privet (Ligustrum ovalifolium *'Aureum'), variegated holly (* Ilex × altaclerensis *'Golden King'), clipped into tiers, and a tawny beech hedge line a grass pathway at Barnsley House. Their shapes, complementing the texture and color of their particular foliage, are distinctive throughout the year.*

A composition of striking foliage plants weaves a tapestry pattern of green, gold, and gray-blue. A golden-leaved elder, Sambucus nigra 'Sutherland's Gold', Bowles' golden carex (Carex elata 'Bowles Golden'), glaucous-leaved hosta (Hosta 'Buckshaw Blue') with dark violet flowers, feathery fennel (Foeniculum vulgare), and Vinca major 'Maculata' are part of a cool scheme in the walled garden at Hadspen.

*A*PRIL

Simplicity Restraint is a fundamental principle of good gardening. Simplicity brings a sense of calm, whereas too many ideas and too much variety creates a feeling of restlessness. Simple schemes involving massed color planting and frequent repetition are usually more effective than complicated compositions and diverse plant associations. In a small garden it is even more important to simplify than in a larger space, doing a few things well rather than a lot less well. Single late tulips (*T.* 'Magier') at Longwood, seen here in close up, are arranged in sweeping patterns to make quietly satisfying visual pictures.

At Wave Hill, native dogwoods flowering in spring above white daffodils shelter a rustic bench and convey a feeling of peace and simplicity. Too many different colors, ideas and features often clutter the scene.

A stone obelisk is framed by giant hundred year-old yew pyramids at Athelhampton. A Renaissance theme comprising gray stonework, green architectural plants, and the occasional flower for emphasis is a classical example of simple gardening. This garden, created in the 1890s, takes its inspiration from earlier centuries.

*Repeated clumps of the regal lily (*Lilium regale*), used throughout a planting scheme at Bettiscombe, in both flowerbeds and in pots, are a unifying feature in the garden. Reliably hardy in the English climate, this scented lily will grow in sun or half shade in most areas of Britain. In areas with late spring frosts, pots of lilies can be plunged into beds and lifted intact for overwintering.*

The Laburnum Tunnel at Barnsley House, seen here from one side, is an important vertical feature, and a color scheme restricted to complementary yellows and mauves reinforces its underlying simplicity. Wisteria flowers between the laburnum chains and tall alliums with spherical heads flourish at the base of the trees

MAY

Creating a Sanctuary Enclosed gardens evoke early ideas of paradise, where walled oases became sanctuaries filled with flowers and sparkling water, a welcome relief from the arid desert outside. Gardeners, through the ages, have sought the elusive idea of seclusion. Today, these inner sanctums can be the whole of a city garden surrounded by high-rise buildings or a secret area in a more generous country garden. In my garden at Bettiscombe, the inner walled area, remote from the outer world, is a private haven. Planted in a relaxed cottage style, the terrace pots provide an opportunity for growing tender plants and annuals.

At Wollerton Old Hall, the garden is divided into enclosures, linked by a series of axial views. Here double borders, roses, catmint, hollyhocks, and silvery artemisias frame an open doorway, inviting exploration or a lure away from paradise.

*In a long vista at Barnsley House,
thick planting frames a distant view
of a sundial, and separates these flowerbeds from the rest of the garden to give
a feeling of remoteness and secrecy.
Large-leaved architectural plants,
in particular biennial archangelica,
give interest in summer.*

A narrowing path and a doorway swathed in flowering climbers suggest a mystery to unravel at Wollerton Old Hall. The smallest gardens can arouse curiosity by using fences, trellis-work, screens, walls, and hedges to create hidden divisions and secret corners.

As gardeners we create peaceful refuges by emulating nature. At the bottom of the garden at Denmans, an excavated water garden is surrounded by lush moisture-loving plants with contrasting foliage shapes. Rafts of water lilies, planted in stone-built containers to prevent them spreading, alternate with more open areas of sky-reflecting water.

JUNE

Visions of Nature As gardeners we manipulate nature, looking at natural plantings in woods and meadows and choosing plants to create our own patterns of color and texture. Consider the relationship of your garden to the surrounding landscape and use the trees and sky, woodland, and hedgerows, the rolling countryside, even fields and meadows, as inspiration. At Bettiscombe, I look out on the Dorset hills, a view which would be spoilt by introducing exotic trees. Instead I emphasize my role as gardener by establishing a framework of yews which defines the garden area and by using my neighbor's trees as part of the design.

In a garden on Chesapeake Bay, designed by Oehme and van Sweden, the view looks out on the ocean, with a foreground planting of massed sedums seen here through the house windows. More naturalistic planting, often of regional natives, can be at the garden perimeter, with exotic introduced plants having a foreign "look" best planted near the house.

At Butterstream, species and "old fashioned" plants make lacy patterns in the closely packed, informal borders. The effects look natural but depend on constant grooming to maintain balanced pictures. Here, yellow daisy flowers contrast with the tall spikes of white Lysimachia ephemerum, *a froth of heart's ease, and thistly* Eryngium giganteum.

In John Brookes' wilder planting areas, he encourages self-seeding. Here random volunteers of foxgloves, cowslips, and forget-me-nots emphasize the natural look at the edge of one of the graveled areas containing grasses, sedges, lupins, and irises. Take more inspiration from nature by allowing drifts of hardy bulbs and wild flowers to colonize in grass and aconites and wood anemones to spread under the canopies of trees.

In the Azalea Woods at Winterthur, shrubs are massed in bold blocks to make a colorful and naturalistic forest scene in spring. Torch azaleas from Japan, which bloom when the foliage is young and light green, are under-planted with ostrich ferns beneath the canopy of tulip poplars and flowering dogwoods.

JULY

A Sense of Order Gardeners work in three dimensions, planting in different planes and using geometry to manipulate area and volume. Like an architect, learn about balance and rhythm as well as proportion, using verticals to fill volumes of space and ground patterns to emphasize the horizontal. In the Nancy Bryan Luce Herb Garden at the New York Botanical Garden, geometric beds edged with boxwood fill the central area, creating a sense of order and peace, with more riotous perennial herbs in the outer borders. The boxwood encloses alternating gravel and flowerbeds, and the essence of this patterned design is control and repetition.

In the newly restored walled gardens at West Dean, cabbages, planted in rows, are backed by tall dahlias. Old-fashioned kitchen garden layouts have a satisfactory rhythm which indulges the logical mind.

At Wollerton Old Hall, an enclosed garden area has a horizontal pattern of boxwood-edged beds, given vertical interest with wooden obelisks and conical evergreens which fill the cubic space as if it were a furnished room.

*In the upper garden at Bettiscombe, the central scheme is very ordered. A copper cylinder planted with lyme grass (*Elymus arenarius) *is visible from most other areas of the garden. A fringe of giant catmint (*Nepeta 'Six Hills Giant'*) surrounds the flowerbeds and a froth of lady's mantle (*Alchemilla mollis*) tumbles down the stone steps which link the levels.*

Rosemary Verey's Potager at Barnsley House is ordered on a geometric system that is both efficient and decorative, with planting on the horizontal level in squares, triangles, and straight rows. Shaped fruit trees and vertical frames give height and the latter provide essential support for annual beans and squashes.

AUGUST

Sunlight and Shadow Contrast of shadow and sunlight gives extra dimensions to a garden – an open glade in a dark wood-land, moving from the shade of a pergola into open sun, and filtered light coming through overhead trees. Remember how light changes during the day as well as through seasons of the the year. At Longwood's Topiary Gardens, the reflection of light on vertical, horizontal, and sloping surfaces, provides lots of visual contrast. The greens of foliage in all their different shades and textures provide a background and foil to the brighter and more ephemeral flowers.

In a shady corner at Bettiscombe, where only the western sun penetrates in the evenings, the contrast between light and shadow is accentuated by the planting, with pale flowers and the leaves of the giant Asian dogwood (Cornus controversa 'Variegata') glowing in the foreground.

At West Dean, the sun's rays pierce through the foliage of a mature smoke bush (Cotinus coggygria) highlighting the airy flowers. Trees and shrubs can be heavy with dense foliage or almost weightless, allowing light to penetrate their structure.

*A wooden pergola, tall hornbeam hedges, and pots create shade patterns at the front of the house at Bettiscombe. In the large containers hardy ostrich plume ferns (*Matteuccia struthiopteris)*, with decorative spring shuttlecocks opening to elegant fronds, catch the midday sun.*

At Athelhampton, a shaft of sunlight through an open doorway emphasizes the contrast between light and shade. Any device which enhances the drama of a situation can be worth employing, but if used too frequently will lose its element of surprise.

SEPTEMBER

A Grammar of Color Color is a major element in garden design but, like a grammar, learn the principles and then remember that, in spite of color theories and rules, most flower colors blend together. Think about the whole picture rather than concentrating on details. Foliage color is more muted and can reflect and share the pigment of flower petals. In my outer garden at Bettiscombe, bronze leaves of dahlias, purple orach, and a giant rhubarb combine with scarlet flowers, small bushes of dark red nasturtiums, and paler opium poppies, which look like scatter cushions among the furniture.

At Hadspen in the cool central border, mainly of greens and pale glimmering yellows, Rosa *'Lichtkönigin Lucia', entwined with golden hop (*Humulus lupulus *'Aureus') stands out against the darker background, dominating the quieter planting of ferny fennel leaves.*

The Asian dogwood (Cornus contro-versa *'Variegata') provides a brilliantly sympathetic background to blue, mauve, and purple-flowered herbaceous plants in Helen Dillon's town garden in Dublin. Helen's "blue" border ranges from pale to dark shades, but all the flowers have traces of blue pigment which unite the design.*

In the red border at Hadspen, scarlet-flowered Dahlia *'Ellen Houston'*, Crocosmia *'Lucifer', and red nasturtiums on the wall are set off by bronze foliage. Overall color effects are more important than the detail of individual color associations.*

*At Barnsley House in spring, tulips and cowslips pierce through the foliage of a stinking hellebore (*Helleborus foetidus*) to create the impression of a yellow flower meadow. Effects such as these, in which flowers and leaves are combined, need plenty of forethought and meticulous planning. A hint of violet gives sparkle to the scheme.*

OCTOBER

Reach for the Sky Verticals in the garden, either trees or structures, draw the eye upward and fill the empty volumes of central space. Then the sky in all its seasonal moods becomes part of the design. In my new garden inside the walls at Bettiscombe, I have used globe locusts (*Robinia pseudoacacia* 'Umbraculifera'), which grow as standards, and a series of arches, entwined with roses and clematis, to give height and interest. A further bonus of vertical plants is that they encourage birds to come into your garden.

At West Dean, the gigantic pergola designed by Sir Harold Peto stretches across the upper garden, giving structural drama to the garden landscape. Roses and clematis clothe the pillars above borders filled with plants tolerant of half-shade.

A metal wigwam, finished with a turned wood finial, makes a strong vertical statement, silhouetted against the sky. Used as an architectural feature or as a climbing frame for clematis, beans, nasturtiums, or hops, these man-made constructions are alternatives to living plants. At Bettiscombe, I have a pair of these wigwams in my outer border on which I grow different plants each year.

Herbaceous plants – verbascums, giant thistles, hollyhocks, evening primroses, and giant tobacco plants – all have soaring stems topped with flower spikes and can be used as dramatic features among more rounded shapes and forms. At Wave Hill, pale hollyhocks provide some of these vertical accents.

At Barnsley House, annual sunflowers peer over the top of Rosemary Verey's "apple tunnel", a structure which adds height and interest to her Potager. Nasturtiums wind their way up the frame and around the sunflower stems, with surplus lettuce seedlings allowed to bolt so their darker foliage makes a good foil to the nasturtiums.

November

Appropriate Planting All species plants, wild plants, are native to somewhere in the world. Those that originate in similar habitats will thrive and look right together when planted in the garden. The gardener can choose plants suitable for the site: Mediterranean plants for dry stony soils, plants from damp valleys for rich moist soil, and so on. On the upper level of my inner garden at Bettiscombe, Mediterranean-type plants, all of which require hot sun and good drainage, thrive together, dominated by the golden stems and flowers of *Stipa gigantea*, a grass from the mountains of the Iberian peninsula.

At Hadspen, the giant-leaved Gunnera manicata *from south Brazil looks right beside the water. Thriving in marshy ground where it is hardy, it is an unequaled landscape plant, its crowns protected in winter by the dead foliage. Plants such as these can grow happily and look natural beside artificial water features as long as enough moisture is provided.*

*At Winterthur, hardy plants from
all over the world look right planted
together if they find the conditions
they need. Here, in acid soil, exotic
red azaleas from Asia flourish
under the canopies of tall tulip
poplars (*Liriodendron tulipifera*),
with the native spring blooming
phlox (*Phlox divaricata) making
a blue carpet in spring.*

At Denmans, John Brookes encourages self-seeders to make natural flowerbed patterns. Biennial angelicas, sisyrinchiums, and verbascums all germinate in the well-drained gravel and are backed by the elegant plumes of the accommodating goat's beard, Aruncus dioicus, *which thrives in any soil in dry or moist situations.*

At Mottisfont, Mediterranean-type plants, all of which require sunshine and excellent drainage, thrive together in the open borders. For most perennials it is quite possible to manipulate the border conditions to suit the type of plants chosen.

DECEMBER

Framing the View Carefully framed views and vistas are important elements in garden design. Views are nearly always improved if they are narrowed so that the eye concentrates rather than roams. Trees not only frame a landscape but, most importantly, shape the skyline. On a smaller scale, shrubs flank the edges of a pathway or define a gateway, and double flower borders can have a focal framed point at the end of the vista. At Athelhampton, panels of grass and dark yews frame the canal, with pots marking the four corners to reinforce the symmetry and emphasize the gardener's mastery over nature.

At Mottisfont, clipped yews surround a central pond and double borders stretch to the distant doorway, framed by another pair of dark yews. Even a pair of gateposts or decorative pots can be used to narrow a view and achieve an element of concentration.

A rustic arch in living beech frames the east face of the Tudor house at Wollerton Old Hall. Conical clipped trees flanking central topiary draw the eye to the end of the vista terminated by the facade.

DECEMBER *week 3*   *Framing the View*

*Rosemary Verey's Yew Walk narrows
the perspective to frame the iron gate at
the end of the vista. Helianthemums,
which only open their flowers when the
sun shines, grow in cracks between the
paving stones to make a ribbon of color
between the yew trees (*Taxus baccata
'Fastigiata').

At Wollerton Old Hall, an arch in the brick wall reveals a statue placed as a focal point in the flowerbed. Yellow and white flowers link the two areas, making the transition between the sections of the garden as gentle as possible. In planting schemes, repetition, used to define a vista, edge a path, or outline a gateway concentrates the eye as effectually as using color repeats in border schemes.

Author's Acknowledgments

Working with Janis Blackschleger on Perennial Productions' television series "The Art & Practice of Gardening" gave me an opportunity to visit many wonderful gardens, some of which are featured in this journal. My thanks go to all the owners who made their gardens accessible, to everyone who contributed to the series, and to all the people who worked behind the scenes to make it worthwhile and fun. I would also like to thank Erica Hunningher for working with me on this journal

The Gardens

Athelhampton, Dorset
Barnsley House (Rosemary Verey), Gloucestershire
Bettiscombe (Penelope Hobhouse), Dorset
Butterstream (Jim Reynolds), Co. Meath
Denmans (John Brookes), Sussex
Forde Abbey, Dorset
Gwaltney (Oehme/van Sweden), Maryland
Hadspen (Sandra and Nori Pope), Somerset
Longwood Gardens (Rick Darke), Pennsylvania
Mottisfont Abbey, Hampshire
The New York Botanical Garden in the Bronx, NYC
Town garden (Helen Dillon), Dublin
Wave Hill (Marco Polo Stufano), New York
West Dean (Jim Buckland and Sarah Wain), Sussex
Winterthur (Tom Buchter), Delaware
Wollerton Old Hall, Shropshire

The Photographs

Ted Betz front cover (Longwood Gardens), half title page (Bettiscombe), frontispiece, January weeks 1 and 2, February week 4, March principle and week 1, April principle, weeks 2 and 3, July principle and week 1, August weeks 1, 2 and 4, September weeks 1 and 2, October weeks 1, 2, and 3, November week 2, December principle, this page (Longwood Gardens), back cover
Jerry Harpur facing copyright page, January principle, weeks 3 and 4, February week 1, May weeks 1 and 3, June week 1, July week 2, August principle, November week 3, December week 3
Jacqui Hurst © FLL June week 2
Andrew Lawson February principle and week 3, March week 3 © FLL, April week 1, May principle and week 2, June principle, weeks 3 and 4, July week 3, August week 3, September principle, October principle, November principle and week 1, December week 4
Tony Lord May week 4, July week 4, October week 4, December week 1
Clive Nichols February week 2, March weeks 2 and 4, April week 4, September weeks 3 and 4, November week 4, December week 2